The Secrets of Elemental Quilting

KAREN McTAVISH

On-Word Bound Books
innovative publishing
DULUTH, MINNESOTA

Photo Credits:
Karen's bio pic: Steve Tiggman from Jeff Frey & Assoc. / Duluth, MN
Cover and all other photos: On-Word Bound Books / Duluth, MN

Printed in the United States of America by Service Printers of Duluth, Inc. / Duluth, MN

DVD replication done in the United States of America by North Street Media / Indianapolis, IN

Published by On-Word Bound Books LLC. / 803 East 5th St./ Duluth, Minnesota 55805
http:/www.onwordboundbooks.com/

ISBN 0-9744706-2-7

10 9 8 7 6 5 4 3 2 1

With love to my son, Storm Joseph Krause,

and in loving memory of Joanne Larson Line.

© Copyright Use and This Book ©

Thanks to my editor and publisher, Sara and Dave, for making my chicken scratch drawings look so professional. I have no clue how you did it but I know it was a lot of work. A special thanks to Airtex Batting and Superior Threads for your support with all my endeavors. Thank you to APQS quilting machines for making such great machines, which in turn, make me look really good. Thank you to Sew Batik for your wide width batik fabrics which are perfect for wholecloth and shadow trapunto.

TABLE OF CONTENTS

Introduction

I have created some fun and unusual quilting designs to enhance today's quilts. (Perhaps you have already checked out some of the designs in this book.) Each design has its own spin on the quilting tradition – usually "outside" the box. I tried to keep the integrity of traditional quilting but sometimes I just went crazy with the creative process. The quilting designs in this book are meant to inspire you to show off the quilting more than the piecing of a quilt. My quilting ethic tells me that my philosophy is wrong here; but when it comes to quilting on plain fabric in a block, border, or wholecloth, nothing sings louder than some fabulous quilting designs. I love to see a great motif on a quilt. My eye wanders around the quilt seeing the same element in different poses or modified in new ways all over the quilt.

Each quilting motif in this book is designed as an element. This means that by combining an element in many different ways you will come up with a unique design with elegant continuity. Some of the motifs are elaborate, which means more work on your end, and some are simple and continuous. Either way, you will be inspired to get busy quilting no matter what style of quilting you are into.

In addition to the elemental designs in the book, I have added a great DVD with a lesson on the how-to's of trapunto, shadow trapunto and color trapunto using a design from the book. This is cutting edge trapunto for today's quilter - literally. These new techniques in trapunto will also get you out of any creative

slump you may be experiencing - just watch the step-by-step DVD and you'll be ready to get going again. Any quilter can enjoy this book and DVD whether a hand or machine quilter. If you are passionate about quilting, and you want to be keyed up instead of burned out….then this is the quilting book for you.

Secrets Revealed

I will search high and low for a quilting idea that makes me feel obsessive about the quilt I am working on - one design that speaks to me. I often look outside of the quilting world for inspiration. I look for ideas anywhere from architecture to copyright-free tattoo art. If it's a great design, even if it's out of a motorcycle maintenance handbook, I will buy the book for the sole purpose of incorporating the design into a quilt. (I wouldn't be surprised if the tattoo industry uses some of the motifs in this book, or if someone uses the designs in stenciling walls or furniture.)

When I find a design that I love, it is usually not the right size for the quilt. To get the right size, I will take the design to a copy center for enlargement or reduction. I'll make several different copies, enlarging or reducing by percentages. For example, I might enlarge a design by 30%, 50% and 75%. Then I'll take it home, audition each size, and figure out which one works in my quilt. When the design is the right size it's easy to transfer it to the quilt by marking directly on the fabric, using a light box or transferring the design from the back of the quilt.

If I am creating my own pattern, I start with a piece of paper and a pencil. I play with lines and swirls until I can see the motif come together. When I am happy with my design, I trace over the pencil lines with a permanent ink black pen. The motif will be dark enough now so I can see it through the fabric and mark the quilt top.

I love stencils but I try not to buy too many because quilt show judges are pretty familiar with most traditional quilting stencils on the market. They want to see something new, fun and original. Luckily, I enjoy drawing out my own quilting designs which makes the quilt "one of a kind." When I design my own quilting elements I want the judges to say, "Hey! That's something I have never seen before, that must be original!" Chances are much higher to ribbon on a quilt with original quilting designs.

I use water soluble or air soluble marking tools to mark my design directly onto the quilt top. These products will come out of the quilt with little or no effort. I only mark a quilt top with water soluble pen if I know that the fabrics are washed, so when I submerge the quilt in water to get rid of the markings, the fabrics will not bleed. I like to use the purple air erase pen, but the ink only lasts about 24 hours before the marking starts to fade. If I'm not using trapunto the purple pen is great. When I am using trapunto in a quilting motif, the purple pen is not an option. I then will use a blue marking pen, such as "Mark-B-Gone" or a chalk pencil or chalk pounce pad. It is important that the chalk lines are not rubbed off or faded when using trapunto. You need to see your motifs until the final quilting stage is completed.

When I have my marking tools ready, I find tracing the designs easiest from under the quilt. If it is too difficult to see the quilting motif, I will use a light box.

Trapunto is a huge part of exposing the beauty of elemental quilting design. The motifs won't be as thunderous without trapunto. It's important to remember, when making the decision to use trapunto, that all that trimming will be worth it in the end. Take it from me, there is nothing worse than designing a fabulous center piece quilting design, skipping the trapunto and then not being able to see the design at all because it blended into the fabric without any loft. Makes you want to cry. Been there, done that. Not fun.

Making a quilting design decision can only be done by auditioning several designs against the quilt top. Your gut will tell you if it works or doesn't work. You will know instinctively when a design is too complex for the quilt top. If I am unhappy about my quilting design decisions, I tend not to be proud of my work in the quilt and it may not ribbon well in shows. As long as I am in love with the quilting elements I picked, I know I will get the quilt done and it will look great.

Once you pick your main motif, work other elements of the design into the quilt top too. You can use the same element, combined in new ways, in the center blocks, on-point blocks and corners. The design, if slightly altered and added to, will also look great incorporated in the border. Remember, do the hardest thing and push yourself – it always pays off in the end. ✑

Using Elements

What is the secret to elemental quilting?

Here is the element, Excaliber, in purple.   I flipped the element and drew the reflection.

See how one element repeated four times at different angles creates a pleasing border. This is the design used in the DVD.

The main secret is to use a single element or motif to create a design you could never have imagined. Basically, the single motif or element is made into many different designs by twisting, turning, flipping, reversing and modifying the design. You can even create new designs by combining one part of one element and one part of another element. By auditioning the element you choose for your quilting design under the quilt top, you can tell how much to enlarge the design, and if you need the mirror image of the design. You can add any of the motifs into a block, they can stand alone like an Ohio Star, or you can repeat the design into a border. Using the patterns in plain fabrics makes the designs stand out even more, but what really grabs your attention is adding trapunto to the quilted element.

There are several fabric marking tools out there. Find what works best for you by asking your local quilt shop which marking pens are the safest to use on fabric. The tool I like to use for "un-marking" is the Clover eraser pen. This is great for removing mistakes made by the blue water soluble pen or purple air erase pen. It completely removes the pen marks so you can re-draw your design without having to spray water on the area. The Bruynzeel Chalk Pencil is great for marking on dark fabrics. After I mark a top with it I can easily brush the chalk mark away.

Have many long rulers available to use that will cover the entire length of the block or area you want to quilt in. Then start with a fresh new marking pen so the lines are crisp and bright.

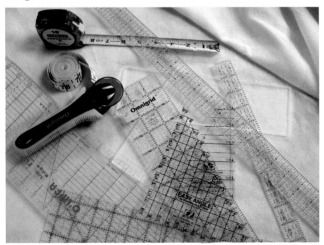

*F*irst, I mark a registration line from corner to corner and center to center.

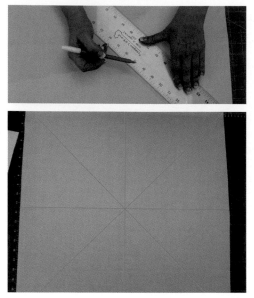

*T*he lines will help me place the motifs in the space correctly. It doesn't matter if this is a wall hanging or a king sized quilt, I always mark the quilt top all the way across. If this were an appliqué or pieced quilt the lines wouldn't be necessary as the pieced or appliquéed areas would dictate where to place the element.

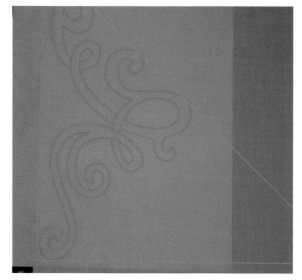

*P*lace the design under the fabric and position the motif so that the tips of the design are just touching the registration marks.

*T*he patterns in this book most likely need to be enlarged, especially if you are choosing to use trapunto. Choose your design and go to the copy center to enlarge it. Make several enlargements, increasing by percentages, such as 30% larger, another copy at 50% larger, another at 80%, and so on until you think you have enough examples to audition. One of the increases should be a perfect fit.

*H*ere I need the mirror image of my motif. I flipped the paper image to the wrong side and traced it from the back with a permanent marker so I could see the line clearly. I used a light box for accuracy. Tracing the image from the back creates a mirror image to match to the opposite corner of my design. The way to mark darker fabrics, including black, is to use a light box. Light boxes are sold in most quilt shops and hobby supply stores.

Here, I am marking the design directly on my block by placing the paper under the fabric. I can see clearly through the fabric so it's easy to use a water soluble marking pen to trace the design. With a steady hand, gently trace around the design then move to the next corner. There is no need to tape down the fabric; if you are gentle with the pen, the fabric should not move.

Instead of copying the back side of the paper pattern I can use the light box to trace the mirror image of my paper design directly on to the fabric.

To take out marking mistakes, use the Clover eraser pen. I redraw the correction first, then take out the "oops."

Now that the quilt top is marked I'm ready to do my final quilting or add trapunto. See the Trapunto How-to chapter at the end of the book and watch the enclosed DVD for a lesson. ↩

Fundamental Feathers

If you can learn how to quilt these feathers in a continuous fashion, your work will not only look very professional and well thought out but you will whiz through it at the speed of light. If you are unfamiliar with how to quilt these feathers without stopping and starting, I would suggest buying my book, *Mastering the Art of McTavishing*, with the enclosed DVD. I demonstrate in great detail how the feathers in this book can be quilted freehand - without any marking of any kind. The feather elements are very traditional - perfect for those 30's fabrics, reproduction fabrics, and very traditional quilt tops.

Sydney Opera House

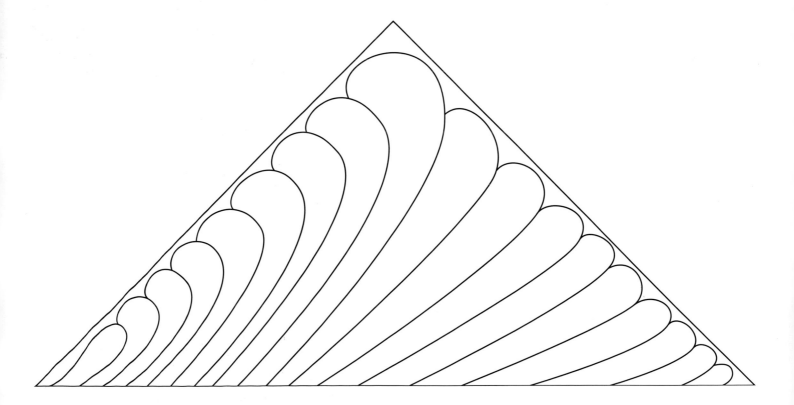

Sydney Opera House used 4 times in a pin-wheel fashion.

Sydney Opera House reflected once to form an on-point block.

Sydney Opera House reflected once, but changed slightly by removing the center dividing line. This creates an entirely new look to this on-point block.

Shooting Plumes

Shooting Plumes used in an upside-down, right-side-up sequence to form a border pattern.

Shooting Plumes reflected 6 times with top points facing each other to form a hexagon block.

Pyramidal Plumes

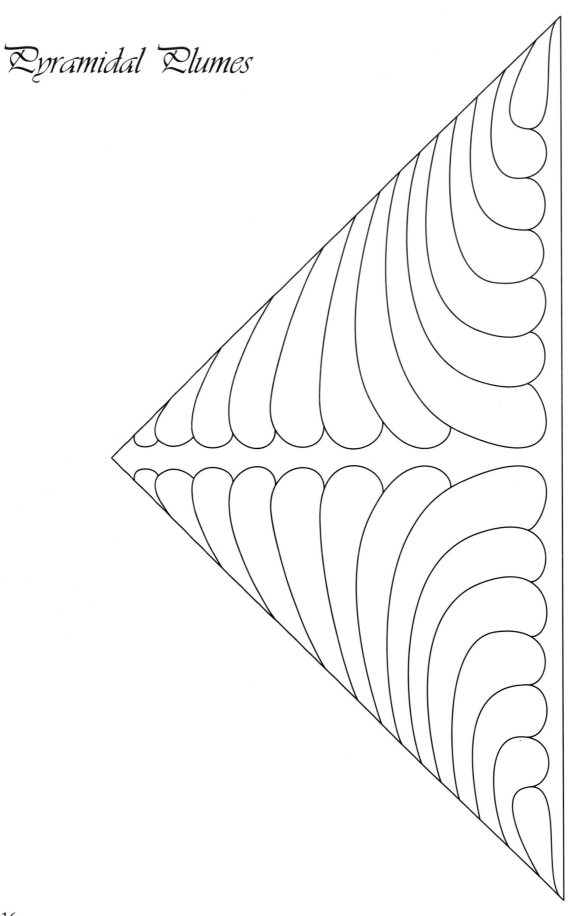

Pyramidal Plumes reflected 4 times with top points facing inward to form a block.

Pyramidal Plumes reflected once with top points facing away to form an on-point block.

Pyramidal Plumes turned, and used once to form a corner.

Pyramidal Feathers

Pyramidal Feathers reflected one time along the bottom to form a diamond block.

Pyramidal Feathers reflected 6 times with top points facing each other to form a hexagon block.

Dove Heart

Dove Heart element rotated and repeated 4 times with the bottom points together for a center motif.

Dove Heart element rotated and repeated 4 times with the bottom points facing out to form a diamond shaped, or on-point, block motif.

Seashells

Sometimes you've just got to have a seashell for the formality of it all. Seashells are the epitome of formal, traditional quilting. You may see seashells in wholecloth quilts as borders or corner plates. They add a little something extra to a quilt - the kind of special stuff that encourages a sharp intake of breath from the viewer. Mission accomplished, baby.

Dropping Feathers

This seashell pattern is so versatile. It can be used alone, as shown above as a corner element, or as an on-point block. Or it can be used in sequence for a border, or perhaps to frame a center design.

$\mathcal{T}$his centerpiece was made by repeating Dropping Feathers 4 times. The points are facing each other giving a nice, rounded look to the overall design.

$\mathcal{A}$nother way to use this motif is as a wholecloth pattern. The size of this pattern would have to be increased quite a bit but it would make a very elegant quilt.

$\mathcal{T}$his is the same design as above, it's just rotated to fit in a block. It's funny how different the same design can look just by turning it a little.

Chinese Foo Dog

𝒯 modified Chinese Foo Dog into a block motif by flipping the element and then joining the loops into one loop as seen above. This design also works well as a single element or as a border motif.

Plumed Shield

Plumed Shield is flipped once then repeated as a set to form an elegant border.

Repeating Plumed Shield 4 times with the points facing towards each other will produce a beautiful design which you can use for a block, centerpiece, or on-point motif.

The Monarch

The Monarch is an eye-catching design by itself or as a corner or border.

These on-point motifs can be rotated 45 degrees to become fancy block fillers. Trapunto could really enhance these designs, but depending on your thread choice they may stand out by themselves.

The Bow

Here's where the elements really start to get interesting. There will be many more options for each element than I can even present. Use your imagination to show you the beauty of making new motifs from a single element. Reflect, turn and combine to your heart's content. Be creative and have fun.

This simple but interesting on-point block is made by reflecting the element along the bottom line of the design.

A larger on-point design can be made by repeating the element 4 times with its top points facing into each other.

This is the same design as just seen but it has been rotated 45 degrees to be used to quilt a block.

You can make The Bow work as a simple corner by aligning its top point to your quilt corner or you can create a more complex corner by using 2 elements and matching the sides together.

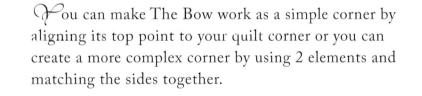

A simple border can be made by repeating the element over and over, touching the tips together for alignment.

A more complex border can be made by inserting an upside-down element between your repeating element.

Victorian Feathers

My favorite thing to quilt is a freehand Victorian Feather. It's fun and never boring. Victorian Feathers are meant to be quilted free hand, with minimal stopping and starting. They are best used in quilts that have a romantic and whimsical feel to them. You may see this style of quilting in toile, floral and shabby chic quilt tops. It's best to use these designs in larger pieced fabrics, such as a large on-point design.

Finite

Finite has so many design options. Here are 2 of the easiest. Finite can be used once for a corner design by facing the long side of the triangle towards the center of your block or quilt, or reflect Finite along the long side of the triangle to make an on-point design that has a feather heart pattern.

By combining Finite 4 times with the long sides of the triangle facing out you can make a slightly more complex block or on-point motif. Both of the corners shown here are elements of the block motif.

This Finite pattern is the most complex. Finite is repeated 8 times to make a block. You will notice that this design is actually the first design (made by reflecting Finite along the long side of the triangle to make an on-point design that has a feather heart pattern) repeated 4 times. By rotating the design you have an on-point pattern as seen below.

Feather Surf

This design is very similar to Finite, but by altering the direction of the feather curl the pattern changes significantly when combining the element.

Reflecting Feather Surf along the long side of the triangle allows a pretty on-point tulip motif to develop.

You can make a crashing wave corner by using 2 Feather Surf elements. Align the long sides of the triangle to the outside edges of your quilt or block corner and face the waves away from each other.

ℐf you prefer a heart corner motif align the long sides of the triangle to the outside edges of your quilt or block corner, but this time let the waves face each other when using 2 Feather Surf elements.

ℱor a slightly more complex block combine 4 Feather Surf elements. If you look at this block you can see both styles of corner contained within it. This block could be rotated 45 degrees for an on-point design. This block could be made even more complex by repeating the design 8 times as shown on the previous design, Finite.

Stiletto

𝒢o to page 97 for a wholecloth sample pattern which uses this border.

𝒩 designed this element to be made into a border. The paired elements could run continuously around an entire quilt or could be used to frame a smaller motif such as a centerpiece or an appliqué block. The left hand example shows the defined corner this element can make too.

Stiletto, made into a centerpiece, is artfully enclosed by a Stiletto border. When you are designing a wholecloth quilt, you can get away with designing the entire quilt with only a few different elements as shown above. Enlarged, this pattern would make a beautiful wholecloth design. It's all about the combination and placement.

A slight feather modification to Stiletto (shown here) provides a variation for your border. Try combining this new design in creative ways to make your own borders, frames and centerpieces.

Cupid's Arrow

$\mathscr{I}$ actually designed this element as a single corner motif. But corner motifs have a way of morphing into other patterns. By placing Cupid's Arrow in a line, arrow point to arrow point, a repeating feather triangle border pattern emerges. By placing two of the top sides together we come up with a double element corner. And then, by reflecting that corner we come up with a block or on-point pattern. I think an interesting frame could be made by placing 4 elements, point to point, around an open square as shown in Stiletto.

Regal

This corner motif is a combination of two other elements, Stiletto and Cupid's Arrow. It's a great example of how to make an entirely new design by combining elements or parts of elements to suit your needs.

By mirroring the element along the top edge and then rotating the new design 90 degrees we come up with an on-point pattern that looks like a stylized feather tree.

Now take your new element, rotate it and repeat it 4 times for a fanciful block. Or turn it on-point for a beautiful centerpiece. This pattern could also be enlarged to make a magnificent wholecloth quilt.

This corner design is another example of how to turn one element into another. Here, I reflected my original element (Regal), but the upper ½ of the design was bigger than the lower ½ so I tucked the reflected "swoosh" under the first "swoosh."

To make this block pattern, I reflected my corner pattern along the bottom edge. You could turn this on-point block 90 degrees so the spiky points are on top, or you could turn it 45 degrees to to make a square block.

Don't be afraid to combine this element many times. Doing the hardest thing always pays off in the end.

This is another pattern that could be enlarged to full size to make a wholecloth quilt.

The Drake

The Drake is an elegant and fairly simple feather element. You can use it alone as a corner or reflect it from either of its flat sides to create a pleasing border as seen here.

Reflecting either of your borders will give you a great feather centerpiece or block filler.

The Chariot

Repeat The Chariot 4 times with the scroll-line in like this to create a decorative frame, or face the scroll-line out as seen below to create an impressive centerpiece. Either of these designs can be rotated 90 degrees to accentuate a rectangular quilt.

Phoenix

This cornerpiece is ½ of the above design. The on-point Phoenix pattern would make a very interesting centerpiece or block filler.

*U*se Phoenix, rotated and repeated 4 times, for a pin-wheel or twisted star pattern. Or just use it to quilt in a block. It's fun, fanciful and quick to quilt.

*P*hoenix, reflected once and stood on its points makes a small on-point block filler.

Seussian

The word "Seussian" comes from my son's Dr. Seuss books. Some of my inspiration seems to be from the books' illustrations or from the craziness of the characters. I like the simplicity of the lines and the easy quilting that these designs offer. These non-traditional designs will work best on bold fabrics, such as batiks, hand dyes, and bright colored quilt tops.

The Lost Scroll

The Lost Scroll is an incredibly versatile element. Here are 2 examples of block fillers and 2 examples of borders. They do look similar but every combination is just a little different. Making the right quilting choice is all about the details. Try combining this element with itself in many different ways to exercise your creativity.

Excalibur

This is the element I used in the DVD. Both the book and the DVD show how to use this design with trapunto, shadow trapunto and color trapunto. (See the Trapunto How-To chapter for details.) I'll show you some other design ideas for this element now. But there are many more options than I can put in the book. This element is even more versatile than The Lost Scroll (previous page).

It's easy to make pretty quilting designs with Excalibur. These 2 block fillers or centerpieces are actually the same pattern: 4 Excaliburs with the big loops pointed together. One is rotated 90 degrees for a new look.

To make this border place Excalibur end to end with the flatter, long side towards the outside edge of your quilt.

This Excalibur design would make a lovely frame for a pieced block, appliqué block or another quilted pattern as shown here. Enlarged, it could also be used as a wholecloth pattern.

There are a number of corner and block designs you can make from this element. Here's one of each to get you started.

Cursive

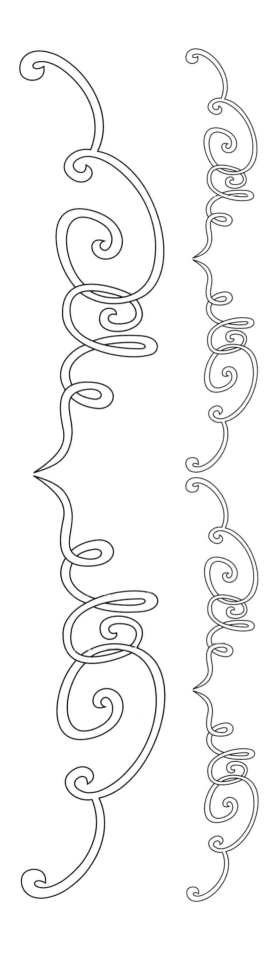

This playful element can be made into a flowing, open feeling border as seen on the left, or a more continuous and compact border as seen on the right.

The two corners you see here are parts of the on-point pattern. If you wanted a cohesive quilting design you could use Cursive in your corners, borders and blocks.

This version of Cursive
would make a really great
appliqué pattern for a
Celtic block quilt.

Chinese Dragon

The Chinese Dragon corner design seen below is repeated in the frame pattern (right) and the block or centerpiece pattern (next page). To make the frame, turn the corner on-point and reflect it.

To make this block pattern use the corner element 4 times as shown.

This border is made by first reflecting Chinese Dragon along its long, more flat side, and then mirroring it along the top or bottom. You could make a simpler border by just reflecting 1 element instead of doubling them up first.

Paradox

Paradox makes a really nice border design. It transitions easily from corner to border as shown here.

You can use this element as a centerpiece or as a double border.

Paradox makes a nice frame too. This design would look great as a stencil on a mirror or picture frame.

Belleville Triplets

Belleville Triplets can be used as a whimsical border, block filler or overall design. Depending on what size you quilt this element it could have the same effect as meandering or stippling except it is much cuter.

These two blocks show how combining this element in different ways can produce unique patterns.

*F*ireworks is a pretty and symmetrical element. It is easy to quilt with its single lines but much more decorative than stippling. A single motif could be used to quilt an on-point design or block, or make a border by placing Fireworks end to end.

A trick I like to use to make a new element is to combine parts. Here, I overlapped the pendant part of the motif to join 2 Firework elements into a single new motif. Then, I just repcat my new pattern to form a border.

Pretty block fillers are easy to form with this element. Try different combinations until you find a pattern that pleases you.

Rotate these block patterns (or the ones you come up with) for an on-point pattern.

Primordial

This is the section where I may have pushed the envelope a bit. My inspiration came totally from the world of tattoo body art. These quilting motifs are labor intensive if you choose to use trapunto. But I always say that what doesn't kill you makes you a really good quilter. If any quilter uses one of these elements in a tattoo design, please send me an email so I can show my parents that I should get one too. It's the only art work we can take to our graves, after all.

Lady Slipper

I designed this element as a corner but with some pattern modification you can make a border too. Simply remove the corner and match up the two sides. You can employ this technique any time you have a corner and would like a border to match.

Quilting this element is quick and continuous. Trapunto would enhance this pattern and really make it pop.

This Celtic looking centerpiece or appliqué block is made using 4 Lady Slipper elements with the corners facing each other.

This border is made by removing the corner of the Lady Slipper element and then joining the 2 sides.

Tear

Tear makes an ornate on-point block design. This would also look good as a frame around an appliqué block.

This easy corner is just 2 Tear elements placed back to back and separated enough to make a 90 degree angle.

This border is made by flipping the element and placing it end to end.

Denizli

Denizli is adapted from Tear. You can do the same thing with any pattern in this book. If you like a part of a pattern but it's not quite right for your quilt, change it a little until it works for you.

This wild block filler/appliqué block/wholecloth centerpiece would really pop with trapunto but boy would it take a lot of trimming. However, if you enlarged the design and used it for a wholecloth quilt pattern, trapunto would be easy and your quilt would really have a unique design.

Venus

This element has three variations. Look on the next two pages if you want to incorporate feathers into this motif.

Venus with Feathers

I've added a second stem to this element to include a sweep of feathers at the top of the motif.

Add a few more feathers to the top of the second stem of Venus with Feathers for another new element. Now, line them up around your borders for a unique look or come up with any other configuration you like.

Caltrop

Try this design by itself, in
a hexagon block or combine
4 Caltrops for an on-point
block (not shown).

Wading Swan

*W*ading Swan, used 8 times (4 pair), makes a very decorative block. You can also use it doubled up as a corner element. This is another motif that would look great with trapunto.

Here is another block pattern
made from 8 Wading Swans this
time with the points facing out.

This border incorporates pairs
of the Wading Swan element to
make an intricate border.

Wholecloth Pattern

Here is an example of a simple but effective wholecloth design. There are only 2 unique elements in this pattern: Stiletto (p. 42) and Dropping Feathers (p. 22). It is the combination and placement that allows this wholecloth design to really sing. For other wholecloth ideas look on pages: 43, 44, 49, 51, 64 and 88.

Basic Trapunto

Trapunto will make any motif scream out to be noticed. This is why it's so great. I do machine trapunto because it's the fastest way to get the effect I want. Originally, trapunto was a hand stuffing method that was very time consuming. Raw pieces of cotton were inserted into the desired area through an incision in the linen backing fabric. When cording was the preferred effect, one would shoot a long trapunto needle, threaded with lengths of yarn, through the middle of the quilting design, leaving little holes in the backing where the needle surfaced. After the trapunto design was finished the quilt could be submerged in water to encourage the holes to close, or the holes could be sewn closed by hand. Today, with the use of water soluble thread, we can achieve the same gorgeous look of hand trapunto but in far less time. I highly advise you to watch the DVD to see a step-by-step example of the stages of trapunto. Like any new technique, it's much easier to understand if you can view the process.

It all starts with something that's invisible.

Vanish is a good water-soluble thread from Superior Threads. If you try to thread your needle by licking your fingers to the thread, you will notice why it got its name. Its use is primarily for basting quilts and for machine trapunto. For larger quilting machines, it is strong enough not to break but thin enough to "go away" in water. I use Vanish as a top thread during the first stages of trapunto. I use a bobbin thread that matches the quilt top - poly blend or cotton is fine.

After loading my machine with Vanish on the top and cotton on the bobbin, I need a good trapunto batting that is really thick. I am very fond of Airtex 16 oz. poly trapunto batting - available at www.airtex.com. This batting is perfect for trapunto - not too thin, not too thick, and fairly easy to snip. This next step stumps a lot of people. You do not need a quilt backing at this time. Yep, no backing is needed. You just have two layers at this stage: the poly trapunto batting and the quilt top. I carefully stitch on top of the blue lines until I have outlined everything that I would like puffy. If your skills at following a line are not so hot, don't worry. By the end of this project you will have greatly improved.

I have taken the quilt off the frame, and the quilt is ready for trimming. The quilt looks like it will pleat at this point because the batting is so lofty. But once the trapunto background is trimmed away and the main quilting is finished, it will lay flat again.

There are several scissors you can use to achieve good trimming, but to get into tight curves and scrolls, you will need a pair of sharp, dangerously pointy scissors. Here are some examples from my stash of embroidery scissors that I use for trapunto trimming.

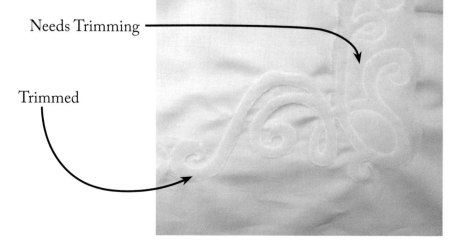

Trim away the batting from the wrong side of the quilt. Trim as closely to the bobbin thread as humanly possible without snipping the quilt top or the bobbin thread itself.

Needs Trimming

Trimmed

Here is the back of the quilt top with trimmed trapunto. Now this piece is ready for quilting with the main batting and backing.

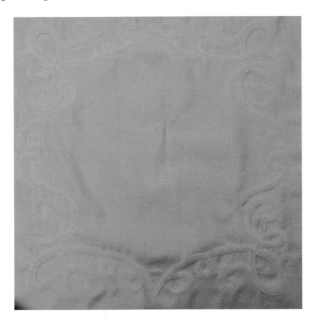

The quilt top still appears wavy after completing the trimming of the trapunto but once the final quilting is done, the quilt will lay flat.

The backing is sandwiched with a very low loft batting, such as Quilters Dream Poly or a flat cotton for the main batting of the quilt. The quilt top is now ready for quilting using a matching thread color. I enjoy using The Bottom Line by Superior Threads for both my top and bobbin thread. It is very fine and shows off the texture of the quilting background filler rather than the stitches.

Backing

Batting

Trapunto batting under the quilt top

Quilt top

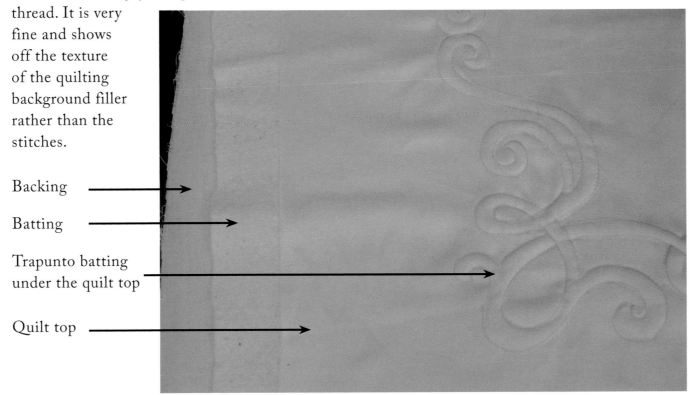

The final quilting is complete and the piece is ready to be dunked in water to remove the water soluble pen markings and the water soluble trapunto thread.

I move the quilt through the warm water until I can see that the blue marks are gone and that the water soluble thread has completely dissolved.

The moment of truth arrives. The quilt just needs to be dried flat and we've got ourselves a finished project. Badda Bing, badda boom, baby. ∾

Shadow Trapunto

Shadow trapunto is similar to basic trapunto but uses different components. First, for your quilt top, you will need batiste or another sheer fabric. Secondly, your trapunto batting should be very white, flat and dense. And third, you will need a piece of really bright fabric–solid or print–that is the same size as your quilt top. Shadow trapunto will turn heads and make people wonder how you achieved such a cool result. Its overall effect should look like dyed batting in the background, but it's really a piece of fabric which is layered in the center of the quilt sandwich, directly under the quilt top. I love to use this style in show. Once a judge wrote on my quilting critique, "Great job on the dyed batting," but it was only fabric – no dyes.

This top is ready for final quilting. The trapunto design has already been marked with water soluble pen and basted with water soluble thread. The trapunto batting is Quilters Dream Poly Request which is very easy to trim away, compared to a high loft batting. Lofty trapunto batting isn't the right choice for batiste and shadow trapunto. We want an unyielding, opaque batting for the trapunto scrollwork. This will allow us to achieve the white cording effect.

Here are some great examples of fabrics suited for shadow trapunto. Some are florescent, some are batiks and some have prints. The sky is the limit on what to use to create a secondary color in shadow trapunto. You could even use neon fleece!

Here is an example of two different fabrics under the quilt top. You can see the pastel colors that the two batiks are producing. Once the final quilting is completed, the color will intensify because the quilting pushes the see-through quilt top and the batik fabric together.

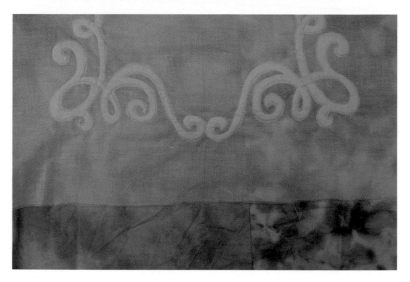

This batik has a nice pattern, and I like the color, but after auditioning it, I didn't think it was very exciting.

Now we're talking! The red is super bright and has a great floral pattern to it. The purple fabric is kind of cool too with its marbled effect, but it's a little muddy looking. When creating a shadow trapunto piece with a batiste top, it is very important to audition your fabric because often what you think will look great doesn't work, and what you might reject could be just right.

This was going to be my choice for this quilt, but I didn't love the after effect. It was just too subtle and I wasn't going for that look here.

Here is my selection for my project, an attractive toile. It's actually upholstery fabric. The final layers for this project go like this:

1. Quilt top with elements marked with blue water soluble pen.
2. Quilters Dream Poly Request trapunto batting, basted with water soluble thread and trimmed away.
3. Bright fabric (under quilt top and trapunto).
4. Flat main batting (under bright fabric).
5. Backing of your choice.

Since I was messing with my machine's tension—using water soluble thread, then switching back to a quilting thread—I ran a little test area before I started to quilt. This enabled me to check and fix any tension problems. Also, I wasn't sure how the batiste would hold up with upholstery fabric under it. Luckily, the batiste was strong enough and didn't shred when I began quilting.

You can see here how important it is to avoid sloppy snipping of the trapunto batting. If you did not trim very close to the bobbin thread, it's going to show up on the quilt. Judges call this "seepage" or "clouding" or "smudging." You may get a comment telling you to "watch your seepage" – which means, in a nutshell, you didn't trim your trapunto batting close enough to the bobbin thread and it looks messy.

After the final quilting is done and we have dunked the quilt project to remove the water soluble thread and the blue pen markings, the toile fabric is clearly visible under the quilt top.

Now it's ready for binding and we are ready to try our hand at Color Trapunto! ❧

Color Trapunto

I came up with this method of Color Trapunto through trial and error after a disaster using dyed batting. I dyed my own wool batting to use for trapunto. I wanted red. When all my trapunto was cut away and the final quilting done, I submerged the quilt in water to remove the water soluble products - and what a mess that was. The entire bathtub turned red when the quilt hit the water. And what else could have turned red?? My quilt. My moment of "TA DA!!" turned into loud screaming of "oh no....oh no....OH NO! No! No!" It wasn't pretty. This was a nightmare that I couldn't wake up from. Anyway, lesson well learned. I went on a search for the perfect product for color trapunto. It could not bleed but it had to be bright in color. I finally found "acrylic" felt. It comes 60 inches wide and can be found very cheaply in most chain store fabric shops. Acrylic felt doesn't bleed, shrink, or beard up, and it is easy to quilt and easy to trim away.

I have my pre-marked batiste quilt top and a piece of red acrylic felt to start my color trapunto project. I baste around the motifs with water soluble thread and trim the extra trapunto away from the quilt top.

*F*or any project using batiste and trapunto, it's critical to trim away the trapunto batting to the best of your ability. Trim the felt as close as you can to the bobbin thread, avoid sloppy cutting, and you will get a nice clean look to your motif. Once the trimming is done, you can quilt the layers together.

*O*ne way to emphasize color trapunto is to use a really white main batting, such as Quilters Dream Poly. After you layer the backing of your choice, quilt away using your favorite white quilting thread. The red acrylic felt will look like appliqué or cording after the final quilting.

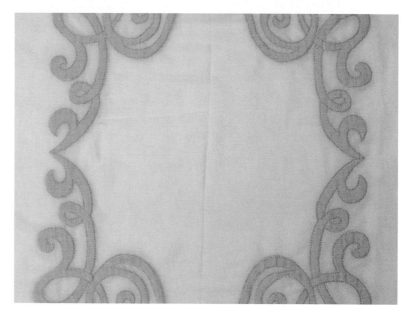

decided to incorporate both shadow trapunto and color trapunto in this project. The trapunto design (color trapunto) is red acrylic felt and the background (shadow trapunto) is a toile print which is layered under the quilt top. All that's left is to quilt the layers together.

Success! After submerging the project in water, the finished piece is great. We have a really easy project here, but it looks complicated. This will really blow some minds on how the heck you did that.

On writing and sketching out this design book, I hoped to offer the quilting world a breath of fresh air. Some of the designs are drawn as a form of therapy to treat quilter burn out. But if you decide that the designs you see in the book are better suited as a tattoo design that's fine too. Just make sure to send me an email of your new body work! Remember - keep your creative doors open and let your quilting flow. ✄

Resources a.k.a. Karen's Favorite Products

Trapunto Batting

Airtex / 150 Industrial Park Road
Cokato, MN 55321
800 851-8887 or 320 286-2428 (fax)
www.airtex.com
Recommended Trapunto batting:
~16 oz. 96" x 11 yd. folded - perfect for all trapunto needs
~20 oz. 96" x 9 yd. folded - great for really lofty trapunto

Main Batting

Quilters Dream Batting / 589 Central Drive
Virginia Beach, VA 23454
888-268-8664
www.quiltersdreambatting.com
Recommended batting:
~Quilter's Dream Poly -3 lofts

Thread

Superior Threads / PO Box 1672
St. George, UT 84771
(800) 499-1777 or (435) 652-1867
www.superiorthreads.com
Recommended Threads:
~The Bottom Line
~Vanish water soluble thread for trapunto

Marking Tools

~Eraser Pen: by Clover
~Blue Water Soluble Pen and Purple Air Erasable Pen (not fine line): Dritz, EZ International, Mark-B-Gone products
~Chalk pencil: Bruynzeel Chalk Pencil #8540866-light gray

Wide Fabrics

SewBatik / 719 Bennett Street / PO Box 365
Portland, ND 58274
www.sewbatik.com
(800) 235-5025

Karen McTavish's Books and Products

www.designerquilts.com
kmctavish@designerquilts.com
(218) 391-8218 (cell)
(218) 525-0017 (phone/fax)

Stencils

McTavishing stencils and pantos:
Golden Threads / 2 S. 373 Seneca Drive
Wheaton, IL 60187
888-477-7718
www.goldenthreads.com

Longarm Quilting Machine

American Professional Quilting Systems
23398 Hwy 30
East Carroll, IA 51401
www.apqs.com
1-800-426-7233

Ruler Templates

The Gadget Girls, LLC
12907 Oak Plaza Drive, Cypress, TX 77429
Phone: 281-890-4222 or 888-844-8537
www.thegadgetgirls.com
Karen prefers these rulers:
~The Little Girl ruler and
~Janet Lee's Favorite ruler

Extend-A-Base and Accessories

Sherry D. Rogers
Runaway Ranch Longarm Quilting Services
19702 8th Avenue
South Des Moines, WA 98148
(206) 878-4720
www.sewfarsewgood.org

About the Author

Longarm machine quilting allows Karen to combine her two passions: Wholecloth and Trapunto. Karen specializes in crafting award-winning quilts using techniques which allow machine quilters to replicate traditional "hand-quilted" effects. She has been featured on PBS's *Quilt Central* and HGTV's *Simply Quilts*. Her work has appeared in Joanne Line's books, *Quilts from the Quilt Makers Gift #1* and *#2*, and numerous national magazines and journals. Karen is the author of *Quilting for Show*, *Whitework Quilting*, and *Mastering the Art of McTavishing*. She has been a full-time professional longarm quilter since 1997 and has been teaching around the country since 2001. Karen lives in Duluth, MN with her family: Dan, Allison and Storm.

Contact her at:
Karen McTavish
Cell: (218) 391-8218
Phone/fax: (218) 525-0017
kmctavish@designerquilts.com
www.designerquilts.com

DVD Table of Contents

Problems with your DVD?

First, try playing your DVD on another DVD player or on your computer. Also, if you are playing your DVD on your computer, make sure you have a DVD drive, not just a CD drive. DVD's and CD's look the same but they are not. If you are having trouble getting the whole DVD to play in sequence on your DVD player, go back to the "main menu" on your DVD and highlight each chapter that you want to view. Not all DVD players will play the DVD from start to finish. If you are having trouble with your audio, play the DVD on a stereo system not a mono system.

This DVD is designed to play from start to finish or in parts. To play a specific section, select the desired lesson from the main menu. This DVD has been formatted to play on NTSC machines in North America. NTSC formatting should work in newer DVD's and TV's from Europe, Australia, New Zealand and Asia as well. If you are from a country which supports PAL formatting, and you can't get the DVD to play, or it plays in black and white, try playing the DVD in your computer or on a newer DVD player with an NTSC compatible TV.

Write to us at contactus@onwordboundbooks.com and let us know if you are having a problem playing your DVD. We will work to resolve the problem and if your DVD is cracked or defective, we will replace it.